# Bringing Out the Sunshine From Within

Janet Guest

Illustrated by Laura Wall

Published by Caseys Court Publishing

*Bringing Out the Sunshine from Within*

Caseys Court Publishing

First Published 2011
By Caseys Court Publishing
All Rights Reserved ©

Email: info@guestwelcome.co.uk

# Table of Contents

The Question of Food     7
True Blue     10
Global Warming?     13
Butterfly Stuff     15
Faceless People     17
A Brand New Dawn     21
If Only Food     23
If All The World Were Chocolate     27
Together     29
Thoughts and Things     30
Truth Or Lies     35
Just Me     37
The Wise Old Man     38
Disillusioned Memories     40
Limerick Lady From Bude     43
The Humble Chocolate Biscuit     45
My Froggy Friend     47
Granite     50
Limerick Young Lady From Bude     53

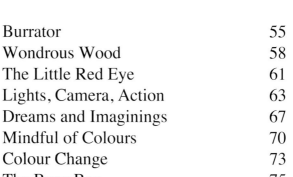

| | |
|---|---|
| Burrator | 55 |
| Wondrous Wood | 58 |
| The Little Red Eye | 61 |
| Lights, Camera, Action | 63 |
| Dreams and Imaginings | 67 |
| Mindful of Colours | 70 |
| Colour Change | 73 |
| The Busy Bee | 75 |
| The Powers That Be | 77 |
| What Shall I do Today | 79 |
| My Teddy Bear | 81 |
| Home Grown Memories | 83 |
| The Very Special Umbrella | 85 |
| 'Tea and Poetry' The Garden Party | 87 |
| Sand Between My Toes | 89 |
| Brave Saint George | 93 |
| The Learning Curve | 94 |
| Poached Eggs on Toast | 95 |
| Happy Christmas | 97 |

# The Question of Food
# To Eat or Not to Eat

You cannot eat the buttercup

Although its name suggests

Nor can you eat the sausage dog

It really isn't best

Be careful of the egg plant

It doesn't have a yolk

You musn't eat its shapely leaves

They would surely make you choke

7

Be wary of the porcupine

Although pork and pine does sound divine

Never eat the cone or spine

Not even with a fine white wine

The hamster may go well with chips

Formed into breaded gourgon strips

Or coated with some tasty dips

But this will never pass my lips

Basil and his brush will not flavour any stew

Nor honeysuckle sweeten any marinated brew

There are of course a few exceptions to the rule

That will really make your taste-buds drool


Like Jacket Potatoes

Toad in the Hole

Beef Wellington or Lemon Sole

Rock Cakes

Cheese Straws

Cat Fish but without the paws

Cottage Pie or Shepherds Pie

That's for you to choose

Make no mistake

When it comes to steak

Just look out for all the clues

# True Blue

I'm sitting in my chair

Having just dyed my hair

Don't stare

It's a great shade of blue

I did it for you

To have a change

Something new

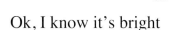

Ok, I know it's bright

But I followed the instructions

I did it right

It said on the packet

It covers all white

Oh, what a sight!

10

I'm not paying hairdressers prices

I'd soon be broke

So I did it myself

Picked it off the shelf

Blue or pink, purple or brown

There were lots to choose from in the town

The blue looked great

Now I've got this state

11

Oh well not to worry

There's no hurry

I'll dye it again

Wash this down the drain

Perhaps purple next time

or maybe lime

The pink might be fun

But it may fade in the sun

Perhaps I'll just stick to my natural shade

Of brown mixed with silver/white

And large patches of grey

The bits of Auburn, quickly fading away

Salt and pepper I think it is called

Maybe I'll shave it all off and go bald

# Global Warming?

I should have been a poet

I knew it from the start

To write my thoughts in song or verse

To tell it from the heart

I could write about the seasons

I know lots of reasons

To start today

I really must begin

The sun is shining brightly

Now don't take this too lightly

Although the day is dawning

It may be due to global warming

Is that a rainbow that I spy?

Faintly colouring the greying sky

Rain must be falling; it's on its way

Oh how I wish the sun would stay

No water shortage for us this year

Although there may be floods I fear

The weather man has had his say

But what will the weather do today

# Butterfly Stuff

Flutter by Butterfly

As graceful as a feather

Flitting here

Settling there

In this sultry weather

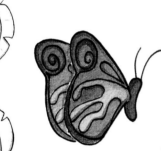

Wings outstretched

Colours glowing

All your radiance

Proudly showing

Flower, tree and leaf are yours

Flying freely or

Stop and pause

A season of sun

To have your own fun

Just long enough

To do butterfly stuff

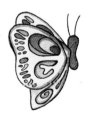

16

# Faceless People

Ivory Towers

White Windows

Pedestals


In the distance

Ivory Tower

People meeting

Every hour

Talking, talking

17

Making a stance

Giving a message

Taking a chance

Ivory Towers

White Windows

Pedestals

Staring out of

White windows

People looking

Friends or foes

Making a difference

Staring, staring

No one caring

Where is your defence?

Ivory Towers

White Windows

Pedestals


People on pedestals

Judging fools

Thinking, thinking

Broken rules

False, illusions

Empty pools

Ivory Towers

White Windows

Pedestals

No advance

Nothing found

Not a sound

Thoughts abound

Tumble, tumble

To the ground

People, fools, illusions

Drowned


Ivory Towers

White Windows

Pedestals

# A Brand New Dawn

We should not spend our lives

What if-ing and regretting

Wishing things would change by all our fretting

'What if I'd tried that?'

'If only I hadn't done that'

We all need to welcome the day

To open our minds in every way

Do all we can to follow a plan

Look to the future

Not live in the past

Life is a journey

Enjoy the moment, don't go too fast

Take time to listen, talk to people, show you care

Don't disregard the voice and views of others

Life is to enjoy, to love and share

Mums, dads, sisters, brothers

Families, friends, our own existence

Generations before us and those not yet born

We can all make a difference

Make your tomorrow, a brand new dawn

My foodie version of the poem 'If' by Rudyard Kipling

# If Only Food

If you can balance your peas on your fork when all
about you

Are losing theirs on the floor

If you can trust yourself with that chocolate cake

And not have a nibble, for your waistline's sake

If you can wait until lunchtime

Without snacking in-between

No cakes or biscuits

No sweets or clotted cream

Or cheese on toast,

Or potatoes; roast

And then stay slim and trim and lean

If you can dream of chocolates and not make your
dreams your master

If you can think of food and not make food your aim

If you can choose from potatoes, rice or pasta

And treat yourself to any just the same


If you can bear to eat the thick and lumpy custard

Poured on by the enthusiastic cook

Or watch while others try to follow exciting, different
recipes from the cookery book

And stop to help by adding just a little mustard

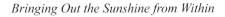

If you can make one heap of all your raw ingredients

And risk mixing altogether in one bowl

And then cook and serve up your concoction

And never breath a word to a single soul

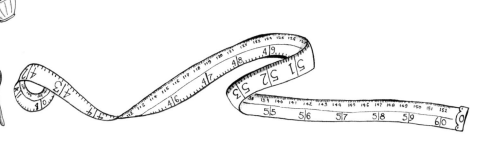

If you can force yourself to eat just one more spoonful

Even though your stomach is shouting out to you it's full

And so avoid your trousers from splitting at the seams

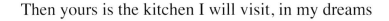

Then yours is the kitchen I will visit, in my dreams

25

If you can talk and eat without getting indigestion

Or walk and not spill gravy down your front

If your cooking is not such a good suggestion

If neither foes nor friends will tell you so, quite blunt

If you enjoy your food as much as I do

With sauces smooth and formed, a perfect roux

Yours is the place I want to eat in

And what is more your food, will not end up in the bin

# If All The World Were Chocolate

If all the world were chocolate

And all the moon were cheese

I'd eat it all in one big gulp

Then fall down on my knees

If all the seas were lemonade

And all the trees were bread

I'd soak them up and drink them down

And then stand on my head

If all the roads were liquorice

And all the buildings fruit

I'd mix the two together

And choose the sweetest route

28

# Together

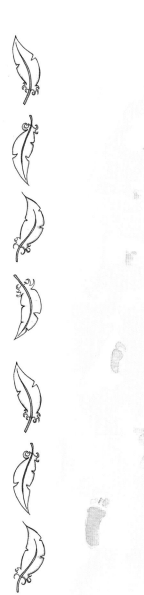

I'll walk with you again

Across the golden sand

I'll walk with you again

And gently hold your hand

Our memories will all unfold

Our future yet to behold

There'll be no tears to cry

Our love will never die

I'll walk along the tide

With you close by my side

We'll live our dreams forever

I wrote this as a tribute to my sister, her name is spelt out in the verses

# Thoughts and Things

Embroidery, Quilting

Crochet, Design

Crafts, Cooking

Gifts, Sewing

All of the above represent Skills


Buttons, Beads

Wool, Silks

Bags, Ribbons,

Felt, Fabric

All of the above represent Hobbies

China cups, Candles

Clothes, Art

Teddy Bears, Leaves

Books, Stationery

All of the above represent Interests

Poetry, Photographs

Words, Walking

Cards, Churches

Treats, Writing

All of the above represent Relaxation

Family, Friends

Wildlife, Gardens

Markets, Themes

Letters, Seeds

All of the above represent Leisure

Exhibitions, Outings, Trips

All of the above represent Events

Skills, Hobbies

Interests, Relaxation

Leisure, Events

All of the above represent You

Kind, Caring

Generous, Giving

Thoughtful, Loving

Talented, Unique

My Wonderful, Special Sister

# Truth or Lies

Truth or lies

Prying accusing eyes

Who can you trust?

No one, but you must

Hide your fears

Hold back the tears


Face another day

Follow the right way

Go with your instinct

Make sure you are not linked

To the politics and rumours

The fakers and assumers

Paving the path

Not considering the aftermath

Not caring of the consequence

Or using any common sense

Just listening to others

Betraying fellow brothers

Lives affected negative

Should be true and positive

Stick to your belief

Don't ponder on the grief

Good will win through

When you stay true to you

# Just Me

First there was me

Just me on my own

Then I met you

And me became two

Together a baby

That made us three

Added one more

That made we four

Husband Wife

Daughter Son

Love binds us together

Forever as one

# The Wise Old Man

We met a man in the old church yard raking up the leaves

We got to talking and admiring the view of the distant hills
and trees

The woods and cops, farmhouses on the moors

Smoke curling from the chimneys

Mist clinging to the tors

A purple hue colouring the scene

Fields of yellow, brown and green

The old man talked of wintry days, memories of the
old fashioned ways

He had worked in the grave yard for many years

And tended the graves with smiles and tears

Wrapped in his scarf, woolly hat and gloves

He knew every flower, shrub and tree

His bright blue eyes sparkled as he asked

"We look but do we really see?"

# Disillusioned Memories

Remember when

Scenes now and then

Misplaced keys

Forgotten Memories

What to wear

People stare

Taking stock

Doors to unlock

Where shall we go?

What do you know?

Views of moorlands

Cliffs, sea and sand

Repeated conversations

Reactions obsessions

Smiles and laughter

Tears and regrets after


Wandering about

A whisper a shout

Mixed up words

Thoughts absurd


llusion Confusion

Dreams retribution

What is real?

How do you feel?

What are you looking for?

What do you see?

I'm looking for someone

I'm looking for me


Listen voices

Content at last

A secret echo of

A forgotten past

# Limerick Lady From Bude

There was an old lady from Bude

Who was always incredibly rude

She poked out her tongue

And thought it great fun

To pull faces and spit out her food

When she went out for a walk

She would not stop to talk

She'd walk quickly away

Then turn back and say

"Get out of my way"

With a squawk

One day she was out in the town

Was given a smile not a frown

She looked at the face

It made her heart race

And turned her rude face upside-down

44

# The Humble Chocolate Biscuit

The humble chocolate biscuit is both a comfort and a treat

The dark ones are appealing and the milk ones always sweet

Still a special biscuit even though we're spoilt for choice

The equivalent in the biscuit world to a classic old Rolls Royce

The humble chocolate biscuit cheers us up when we feel down

It makes us smile and gives us a lift and chases away a frown

Put out a plate of chocolate biscuits and watch them disappear

They are the best above all the rest of that you may have no fear

Other types of biscuits may try to make the grade

But the humble chocolate biscuit is as welcome as any homemade

The humble chocolate biscuit can be eaten anytime

Dunked or eaten on its own

It really is sublime

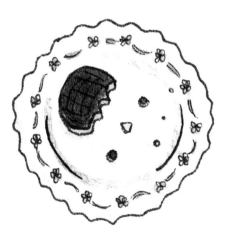

# My Froggy Friend

On the end of my pencil sits a little green frog

He was bought in a foreign land

As you can see by the flag that he holds in his
little green Froggy hand

He was bought by our daughter as a gift,

nearly ten years ago

He wears a beret and a stripy shirt

Not to keep him warm, but for show


He sits on the end of my pencil

Surveying all around from his spot

With other pens and pencils

That I keep on my desk, in a pot

He doesn't appear to have much fun

But is proving to be an inspiration

At night when we're all fast asleep

He hops down from his pencil

And around the place he will creep

He flicks all the paper clips as he hops around

Making Froggy footprints, trying not to make a sound

I've seen the mess he makes when he gets in the filing tray

Mixing up the papers leaving them in disarray

He sometimes hides in the letter rack

Then using the ruler he slides down the back

Hops onto the chair, knowing that from there

He can reach things on the notice board

Pulls on the light cord, swings to and fro

Entertaining his secret friends, putting on a show

My little green frog doesn't live in a pond or a bog

He has never even seen a Water Lily

With his gappy grin and bright green skin

He loves getting into mischief and acting silly

# Granite

Granite is a noble stone

Scattered over moorlands, thrown

Marking roadways, the travelled miles

Fallen, built, neglected piles


Granite, strong, proud

Ivy covered, like a shroud

Standing in forgotten places

Representing many faces


Granite, heavy, bold

Showing stories, never told

Making memories old and new

Churches, headstones are just a few

Granite from another age

Providing men an honest wage

I know not from where this Granite came

But etched into its surface

Find a long forgotten name

Granite boasts a bygone time

A stronger stone than sand or lime

Crafted and hewed by gifted hands

Shipped away to foreign lands

Granite glistening in the sun

Cold to touch, the battle done

Granite with its many traits

Spans across the history dates

# Limerick Young Lady From Bude

There was a young lady from Bude

Who had a really great attitude

She'd laugh and she'd smile for mile after mile

At people she met whilst out walking

One day she went out for a bike ride

Then suddenly started to slide

She flew through the air, which made people stare

But nobody hurried to help her

She landed with such a loud crash

It made everyone scurry and dash

To see what had happened, what damage was done?

But the young lady just shouted

"What fun!"

# Burrator

Narrow lanes our entrance gate

Not enough time to stop or wait

Granite posts mark the way

Across the moorland ponies play

The moss and lichen covered trees

Nothing stirring in the breeze

The water still and icy cold

Surrounded by the dank green mould


Mossy green velvet mounds

Embracing the rough stone strewn grounds

Streams and inlets rushing past

Then slowing down to stop at last


Tree roots hiding under a blanket of green

Making a strange unreal scene

Water gushing from on high

The law of gravity unable to defy

Water racing down the rocky gullies

Light reflecting, changing colours

Clouds scudding across a bright blue sky

Views across fields a bird's eye

Burrator Reservoir our trip out

Gave us lots to think about

# Wondrous Wood

Wooden ceilings

Wooden floors

Wooden walls

Wooden doors

Wooden tables

Wooden chairs

Wooden cupboards

Wooden stairs

Honey coloured

Mottled grain

Smooth and polished

Modest, vain

Different textures

Light, dark

Shaped, carved

Hidden bark

Each piece unique

Grown from seeds

Made to measure

To meet our needs

# The Little Red Eye

It used to be

When I was about three

Before the little LED

We'd turn on the TV


We'd have to wait a little while

To let the tube warm up

The memory of it makes me smile

Sipping from my sentimental cup


The scenes on the screen like magic appear

So bright, in colour and HD clear

24 hours you can make your choice

Watching pictures, hearing a voice

Now there is a constant light

A little red eye in the corner of the room

Changing perspectives, giving insight

That little red eye in the corner of the room

Snippets from childhood memories about different
types of lights, moving through the years

# Lights, Camera, Action

The beams from the search lights crisscrossed the sky,
as they sat huddled together in the shelter.

The candles flickered, making strange shadows dance
on the bare walls. As the wail of the sirens faded
they crept out and stumbled back to their beds.

A red glow lit up the skyline showing the damage done in
the nearby town. The fires raged out of control, lighting
up the night sky swallowing up buildings and people,
showing no mercy.

He sat transfixed, eyes bulging, caught in the glare of the
headlights not knowing which way to run and oblivious of
his fate.

Red, amber green, the car accelerated a kinder way than the
slow death of myxomatosis.

We rushed into the caravan tired but excited, dad lit the
gas lamps and I smelt the familiar smell of the gas
and a slight fustiness of damp, which represented our
long awaited holiday, had begun. The caravan had been
locked up all winter and now it would be our home
for the next couple of weeks. Bedding to be unpacked
and beds to be pulled out and made, a quick check
for earwigs, then a good sleep. We wake up to a bright
sunny day, the start of our holiday.

The lighthouse on the headland blinked out its warning.
It looked romantic and mysterious. One, two, three, blink.
One, two, three, blink.

I didn't really think about its function, to warn of
dangerous rocks for ships. I just took pleasure in the familiar
steady flashing of the light. A friendly presence always
there, always watching, always shining.

I walked along the beach, looking at the millions of
stars, the moon like a big yellow dinner plate, lighting
my way, reflecting in the ripples of the sea.

The screen lit up with a dazzling light as it intruded into
the room bringing  pictures and sounds to our senses
making us feel in awe and inadequate. An unreal
reality to monitor, dictate and dominate our lives.

Mary and Sally are out on the town, they are dancing and giggling into their drinks, the disco lights are flashing all the colours of a rainbow. The strobe lights bounce round the room in time to the music. The UV lights swing into play and reveal more than they should. All too soon the night draws to an end, the lighting is dimmed and the DJ plays his final tune, Mary and Sally have had a great time. The music ends and someone flicks a switch. False daylight in tubes flickers and buzzes above them, cold, white light envelopes them, and the magic is over for another night.

The Christmas tree twinkles with fairy lights the baubles mirror the scene. Brightly coloured presents all carefully wrapped underneath, different shapes and sizes each containing a special gift. There's a smell of cooking from the kitchen and a feeling of anticipation.

Smile everybody, say cheese, a blinding flash from the camera

Another one for the album or to download onto the computer.

# Dreams and Imaginings

I used to get told off at school sometimes for not paying
attention

I enjoyed looking out of the window and day dreaming

Imagining all sorts of wonderful happenings and stories

Scenes and pictures that one day might become reality

I imagined living by the sea,

With children around me

A beautiful house with a few acres of land

Collecting shells, walking along the sand

A simple life

Without pain or strife

Days spent painting or writing a play

Enjoying every minute of my perfect day

Now dreams can come true

It's really up to you

If you keep in your mind

The dreams that you find

Thoughts you had forgotten

Given up on

Pushed aside

There's no need for them to hide

Remember your dreams and imaginings

Think of some really wonderful things

How do you want your life to be?

Just look into your mind and enjoy what you see

It could become your reality

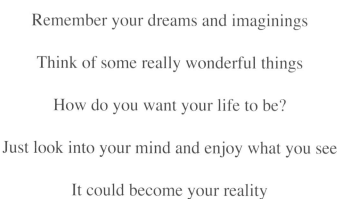

# Mindful of Colours

What would the world be like?

If we only saw in black and white

No bright blue sky

Or trees of green

No colours to enhance the magical scene

Carpets of bluebells would appear a grey haze

Set against a black and white silhouetted maze

A sunset would still be dramatic

But not half so emphatic

Without its warm reds and yellows

One thing that might be better

When dressing to the letter

Everything would co-ordinate

Fashion would rely on variations of pattern and shape

Now wouldn't that be great


Home improvement, decorating

Made much simpler, no hesitating

Colour matching, not necessary

It's the pattern that matters, make light of the task

Black or white I hear you ask

# Colour Change

Colour me orange

Colour me green

Colour me yellow

Picture the scene


Colour me purple

Colour me blue

Colour me red

Follow the clue


Colour me turquoise

Colour me pink

Colour me brown

Hold onto the link

Colour me silver

Colour me cream

Colour me white

Hang onto your dream


Colour me black

Colour me grey

Colour me gold

Welcome each day

# The Busy Bee

Busy buzzy bee

Buzzing round me

Buzzing from tree to tree

Buzzing happy

Buzzing free

Busy buzzy bee

Buzzing round me

Buzzing over by the sea

Buzzing happy

Buzzing free

Busy buzzy bee

Buzzing round me

Busy making golden honey

Buzzing happy

Buzzing free

Busy buzzy bee

Buzzing round me

When the weather is warm and sunny

Buzzing happy

Buzzing free

Busy Buzzy Bee you are the Special Key

(Look after the bumble bee)

# The Powers That Be

It's very irritating

When governments dictating

Telling us what we can and cannot do

   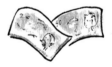

Putting up the VAT

Without a care for you and me

Fuel prices soaring high

Deals for oil in Dubai

Counting costs the Country owes

But still the division grows and grows

Interest rates changing fates

Nothing to spare

It really isn't fair

Who will dare to care?


Bonuses paid to bankers betrayed

Profits turned to loss by HBOS

Markets crash

There's no more cash

Nothing left in the pension pot

Who has got and who has not

# What shall I do today let me see

Dust is building up again

The washing basket is full

The carpet really needs a hoover

The dishes are in the sink

I must wash the floor

I should cut the grass while the weather is fine

That cupboard is in need of a sort out

The car is filthy, full of mud and the inside could do with a clean

It is recycling week must get that out for collection, not to mention the rubbish

I must take that stuff out of the shed, to the tip

Those bags of clothes can go to the charity shop

I can take those when I go up to town

Shopping to get

Tea to prepare and cook

I wonder if I can squeeze those boxes into the loft

Emails to send

Birthday cards to write

Phone calls to make

Lessons to plan

Poems to write

I will have a cuppa then make a start

FATAL

START NOW!!!!!!!!!!!!!!!!!!!!!!!!!!!!!!!!!!!!!!

# My Teddy Bear

My teddy bear is really quite old

When I was little it was him I loved to hold

He brought me comfort and listened to my
stories

As I sat with him cradled comfy on my knees


For a long time now he has sat in his place

Wearing his special jumper with his happy little
face

The other day I was horrified to see

The moths had been eating him for their tea

His jumper is all in tatters

And what is more that matters

They had also been eating his fur

So without his jumper and the fur on his legs,
he is feeling the cold brrrr!!


So poor old ted, with no jumper to wear

His legs all moth eaten, he's looking very bare

But I keep a closer eye on him now, and pat his worn
old head

Because he sits in the corner of the

room just at the foot of

my bed

# Home Grown Memories

It really is a shame

Vegetables just don't taste the same

When I was young I remember the taste

Of carrots and new potatoes, then nothing went to waste

We would sit for hours podding peas

With the bowl balanced precariously on our knees

One for the pot and one to eat

The sweet tasty peas were a real treat

Cauliflowers with their white heads peeping

Marrow fat peas left overnight, steeping

White cabbage, spring greens

Brussels sprouts and runner beans

Carrots to help you to see in the dark

Whether in the street or in the park

Eat up your greens to make your hair curly

It didn't work for me but it did for my sister Shirley

Dad used to grow lettuce, onions and tomatoes

Cucumbers, marrows, turnips and potatoes

Our meals all home grown made such a difference

Certainly I would choose them as my preference

Vegetables bought at the superstore

Sprayed and force grown, imported for sure

With the prices high, and the quality poor

Makes me want to eat less not more

# The Very Special Umbrella

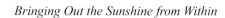

I am a very special umbrella

Although I am not a big seller

You see I don't really keep anyone dry

And I don't even want to try


I enjoy brightening your drink

Can retrieve cherries that sink

I love to twirl round in your cocktail

Though my colourful paper may appear frail

My stick has a point to beware of

So if you're out on the town

I'll make you smile and not frown

I can open and close, but just mind your nose

I stand proud, can delight and entertain

However, I cannot keep you dry in the rain

# 'Tea and Poetry' The Garden Party

I went to a garden party

It was quite a fantastic affair

The lady who ran it was awesome

And made sure there was plenty to share

There were homemade cakes, sausage rolls,

Sandwiches, pastries and more

A harp playing lady entertained us

And there were raffle prizes galore

Everyone dressed for the occasion

Even the weather was kind

More perfect surroundings and company

You'd be very hard pushed to find

So thank you to all who attended

It really was very worthwhile

Here's hoping we meet up again soon

You did it all with such generous style

# Sand Between My Toes

Walking over the headland

I reach for your hand

Slipping and sliding across the sand

I stumble and fall

You walk steady and tall

Exploring the caves

Paddling in the waves

The birds in the distance like notes on a stave

The rock pools glisten

I look and talk, you listen

Through sunshine and showers

We walk for hours

The castle only visible by its towers

The boats all moored tightly

Displaying their colours brightly

Barnacles clinging to the face of the rocks

A touch to their shells and their body sticks and locks

Sand between my toes as I kick off my shoes and socks

Cliffs overhanging giving refuge and sanctuary

Waters meet river, canal and sea

Hermit crabs scuttle to hide,

In the waters deep inside

Their hard shells tested, tried

Different shades of green embellishing the scene, dancing, floating

Seaweed clinging, twisting and turning

The colours always changing, the tides they ebb and flow

There's lots of things to learn about, lots that we don't know

My favourite kind of scenery a never ending show

Urchins, jelly fish, mussels and weed, the silver fish dart

In the underwater world they all play their part

# Brave Saint George

Saint George he was a very brave man

He fought the dragon and made a stand

'No more dragons in this land'

Saint George declared

And in his hand he held his shield

His trusty sword he did wield

The dragon fought with all his might

But it was brave Saint George who won the fight

He slewed the dragon and saved us all

From the dragons fire and a mighty fall

So when Saint George's day comes round

Celebrate in style

But think of brave Saint George

He went that extra mile

93

# The Learning Curve

How steep is your curve

Does it test your nerve?

Will you stay on track?

Or turn your back

Slide and swerve

How long will it last

Will it be short and fast?

Or long and drawn out

Make you want to shout

Tell me what it is all about

Patience needed

Task succeeded

Mission accomplished

Job well done

Now you can go and have some fun

# Poached Eggs On Toast

Poached eggs on toast

I enjoy them as much as a Sunday roast

I had them for breakfast when I was small

Dad used to say 'they will make you grow tall'

'One egg or two' was the familiar cry

'Two please' was always my swift reply

A pinch of salt and pepper to taste

Made sure nothing went to waste

As I cut into the eggs the yolk melts out

The golden colour makes me want to shout

'Hooray!' for the egg, it really is the best

Versatile and tasty, stands up to the test

Have them for breakfast lunch or tea

Or a snack in between that's great for me

Poached eggs on toast there is no taste like it

Fried, boiled, or scrambled, poached is still my
absolute favourite

# Happy Christmas

Happy Christmas one and all

Tonight we're going to have a Ball

Get dressed up and have some fun

Music and dancing for everyone

The decorations, the glitter and the lights

The Christmas tree decked

The gifts and late nights

With lots of food

For the festive mood

Stockings filled

The night is chilled

We celebrate until the dawn

Thinking what Christmas is really about

Remembering the day that Jesus was born

The next few pages are for you to
fill with your own thoughts and feelings.

Happy Writing!

*Bringing Out the Sunshine from Within*

*Bringing Out the Sunshine from Within*